# POWER
# LEARNING

JOHN HUFFMAN

POWER LEARNING

Bennett books may be ordered through booksellers or by contacting:

Bennett Media and Marketing
1603 Capitol Ave., Suite 310 A233
Cheyenne, WY 82001
www.thebennettmediaandmarketing.com
Phone: 1-307-202-9292

ISBN: 978-1-957114-61-3 (Paperback)
ISBN: 978-1-957114-62-0 (eBook)

Printed in the United States of America

Bennett Media rev. date: 02/23/2023

# CONTENTS

# FOREWORD

We live in an information age. Mankind's pool of knowledge grows every year at an astonishing rate. Today computers put facts and statistics literally at our finger tips. More than ever before we have a need to be able to process this information and retain it.

This book is an endeavor to provide the reader with the tools that can help him read better, think better, communicate better, and remember better. If you are serious about improving your ability to learn. *Power Learning* can change your life.

# 1.

# ASSOCIATION BY DESIGN

The memory is a fascinating subject! The important thing to remember at the outset of this chapter is that you can improve your ability to remember! To train your memory you will have to learn how to focus your entire attention on what you wish to learn. This will be easy once you understand the technique for consciously making associations between, even seemingly unrelated, ideas. In this chapter I will show you the foundational concept of association and how you can use it to focus your attention on whatever you desire to learn.

## OUR NATURAL MEMORY

Our natural memory is remarkable! These techniques will not be a substitute for our natural memory. Far from it! These techniques will greatly enhance our natural memory faculty and allow you to do things you would never have thought possible before learning these techniques.

It helps to organize material to be remembered. It is much easier to remember data which is in a logical form or placed under categories. These techniques will enable you to quickly learn and remember the main points of what you need to learn. The details should be remembered through your natural memory. I want to emphasize this! It will save you time in the long run. You will also find that your natural memory will improve automatically as you employ these techniques in this manner.

We unconsciously make associations between things all the time, but now you must learn to consciously and deliberately make associations to burn ideas and facts into your mind.

## MUST BE PICTURABLE

The problem with most ideas is that they are abstract, that is to say, they lack meaning to us. An abstract word or term cannot be pictured as it is. Our minds are, for the most part, eye-minded. We tend to recall better the things we see rather than just hear. So, what we need to do to resolve this problem that hinders our ability to remember is to create an image that will represent that idea or term in our minds. We must make abstract words and ideas picturable. We must make a vivid image.

Take the word "peace", for instance. If this were a word in a list of ten that you needed to remember in a specific order, and the rest were as abstract as this one, you would probably find it difficult. I am sure that you would eventually be able to do it, but only after repeating the list a number of times.

Fortunately, there is a much better way to learn abstract material like this. Allow me to illustrate the principle of converting an abstract word into a vivid image that would represent its meaning. For the sake of simplicity at this stage let's just work with two abstract words and associate them together using this principle. The two words we will use are "peace" and "inflation".

We will symbolize them by a dove and a red balloon on a string, respectively. We are using a dove because that is a common symbol for peace that is already in our minds. The red balloon is used since it will remind us of the idea of being inflated. Inflated in turn will remind us of inflation.

As I describe this picture of these unrelated ideas, try very hard to visualize it. See vividly all of the details that I mention. Here is our picture. There is a red inflated balloon rising into the air and a white dove flies over to it. The dove hovers about it, pecking at it with its beak that is long and looks more like a silver spike than a beak. The dove is huge while the balloon is about the size of a basketball.

Look away from the book for a moment and really see this picture. See the interaction between the dove and the balloon. To help with your concentration on this, or any association, get in the habit of thinking to yourself with questions about it. For example, what is pecking on the red balloon? The answer, of course, would be a dove. Another question: what kind of beak does this dove have? What is the dove doing with it? These questions will simply help you focus your attention on the various details of the picture. I am explaining this to you now not because it is needed here but because it will be very useful in more detailed, more complex pictures, or associations, that we will develop later in other chapters.

This association was made by joining these two images together in one picture in an unusual manner. It is very important to make your images unusual in some way. Here I chose to make the dove unusually large with an unusual beak. You could even visualize the balloon exploding as the beak is thrust into it viciously.

## MAKING IT UNUSUAL

An image can be made to appear unusual in several ways. Let me go over these with you briefly so that you can get a feel for making unusual associations that will be more easily remembered.

You can put action into the picture. In this picture we utilized action when we saw the dove hovering with its wings fluttering violently. We put action into the picture when we caused the dove to thrust its beak viciously at the balloon. I also mentioned that we could have caused the balloon to explode when the beak penetrated it. All of these ideas are examples of how to introduce action into the picture to help you better recall it.

I feel that I must mention here that I am using this example to show you that many things can be done to a simple picture, even when it is composed basically of only two elements or images. This is not intended to imply that you should use several of these ideas for making every picture unusual. Many times, only one of these ideas will be needed to make the picture significantly unusual.

The first way then is to put some type of action into your association. Another way to make the association unusual would be to see the image larger or smaller than it normally would be. This was illustrated in our example by saying that the dove was huge. A dove is never huge in reality, but, when thought of in that way in this picture, it makes the picture unusual. As a result, this picture will stand out in your mind and be easily remembered.

A third way to make your picture unusual would be to use exaggeration. How could we have used this method in our example? We could have included thousands of doves instead of just the one. We could have easily visualized thousands of doves attacking this little red balloon from all sides. This certainly would have made the picture unusual and would have impressed it on our minds for easy recall.

Finally, an interesting way to make an image unusual would be to substitute one of the images. We could have visualized a large, white dove swelling as it rose into the blue sky with a string hanging from its feet like a string would hang from a balloon rising into the air with the wind blowing. Here you see the dove, but the balloon is implied by the dangling string and the action of the image of the dove swelling as if inflating itself.

With this knowledge of how to consciously make associations between abstract concepts and even totally different, unrelated items, you should realize that you are well on your way to being able to learn and remember any kind of material. You will be able to recall facts, dates, a list of things to do, or a list of U.S. Presidents and what years they served in this office. You will be able to sit down and read a magazine article and recall all of the main points and related details. Think of the potential you could achieve! It may enable you to get that college degree or a better job. You will truly be able to accomplish much more than you ever have before and you will be able to do it faster. Read on to acquire a mind that can absorb information like a sponge absorbs water.

## THREE MEMORY TECHNIQUES

Before I get into a detailed discussion of memory techniques and their applications, let me say that there are three basic memory techniques that employ this concept of association.

The first technique is to work with two or more images in one picture. We just used this technique when we associated the two images of a dove and a balloon. We will use it to learn names of people and facts about them in chapter two. This is used for grouping any number of images together when no precise order is required.

The second technique is often referred to as "the chain method". This technique is used when you need to remember items in a sequence. I will briefly explain it here but later I will give you a detailed explanation. You must associate the first two images together in an unusual manner. Secondly, you will need to associate the second image with the third image in an unusual way. After completing this step simply continue until all of your items have been associated to the previous item. You will then have a chain of items that can be recalled forwards and backwards.

The third memory technique that we will discuss in chapter four is commonly referred to as "the peg system". It consists of a phonetic alphabet and numerical equivalents. By utilizing this technique, you will be able to learn enormous amounts of information in and out of order. In other words, you will be able to learn data in a sequence so that you can recall it backwards and forwards, and you will also be able to access any particular item of this information at any time and instantly know its rank numerically in the entire list of this data. As you can see it can be used very well for remembering charts and tables of all kinds. Also, it is an invaluable tool in recalling the outline of a book chapter or magazine article.

Now that you have a good overall understanding of this foundational concept of association, let us go into a more thorough discussion of how each of these techniques using association can be applied.

# 2.
# THE ONE PICTURE METHOD

The first technique for using associations that we would like to discuss is the One Picture Method. The One Picture Method consists of placing in association two or more ideas or facts represented by images in one picture. This concept is very helpful for students learning a lot of material from a textbook. Let me explain the principles for using the technique and then I will show you an example.

The first step would be to create an image that would represent the subject matter or basic idea. Next, you would want to make an image representative of the facts about this subject. Create an unusual image for each idea to be in this picture. Now associate the image of the first fact to this image of the subject.

You then place the image for the next fact in the picture so as to associate it either to the first fact or to the subject image. The reason that you can do this is because there is no order involved. You use this technique just to group facts about a particular subject.

You may continue adding other facts as needed. Just associate each additional fact either to a fact included in the picture or to the subject image. When you think of the subject image you will automatically see all the related facts in the same picture.

## IMAGE FOR SUBJECT

For an example let us say that you are studying biology and that the chapter deals with the central nervous system. Among some of the things that you might want to learn would be the types of neurons. Briefly you would have to learn that Sensory neurons are responsible for transmitting impulses to what are called receptors; that Motor neurons transmit impulses to effectors; and finally, that Interneurons transmit impulses from Sensory neurons to Motor neurons and to other Interneurons.

Following our guidelines above, we will make an image to represent the subject term, neurons. Remember this image can be of something that symbolizes it or sounds similar. A Fig Newton comes to my mind. Newton — neuron. Be sure to make this image unusual! See a rather tall Fig Newton with fig hair and a face. It has large eyes — a lot of the white area showing. Think when making up unusual images as if you were creating a cartoon figure out of an object.

## IMAGES FOR FACTS

Let us think up an unusual image to represent each factual item. For the Sensory neuron let us use a dime. Ten cents — sensory. Again, we will make it unusual in size. Let us make it rather large in comparison to the other objects that we will place in our picture. For a Motor neuron, let us use a motor - a car motor with the fan blades spinning. That will make it unusual. Finally, we can use a doorway with the word "Enter" above it to signify an Interneuron. Now we have all of the images that represent all of the facts that we want to associate to the subject neuron.

Putting all of these images together in one picture is our next step. We can associate the Fig Newton with the dime and the motor this way. See the tall Fig Newton placing a large dime into the car motor like a child would place a coin in a piggy bank. Next, add the doorway with the word "Enter" into the picture and we will have it. See the door frame around the tall Fig Newton. The Fig Newton is standing in it. Now we have the subject image and all three main item images in one unusual picture. The thought of any one image will necessarily bring to mind the entire picture containing all of the images.

## LEARNING THROUGH MEDITATION

In remembering the functions of each of the three neurons, simply use your natural memory. Why waste time thinking up more images when your natural memory will do the job nicely? If you find material of a more difficult context, certainly use additional images for what needs to be recalled.

When you have completed this unusual picture, you need to meditate, or talk to yourself, about what the meaning of it is. Always see the images while meditating but never say what you see while meditating. Always say what they represent and the meaning of any details that these images help you recall.

In this case you see the picture as you converse with yourself about the information to be learned. Tell yourself about the three types of neurons. Continue thinking to yourself, first of all, about how the Sensory neurons work. Recall from your reading what a dendrite is and what the cell body does. Talk to yourself about how this dendrite functions in relation to this sensory cell body. There is also another fiber that transmits impulses away from the sensory cell body. It is called an axon. Whatever you feel is an important detail related to the Sensory neuron should be included in your meditation of this idea which was represented in your mental picture.

After meditating in this fashion about the details concerning the Sensory neuron, begin meditating in the same way about the Motor neurons and finally about the Interneurons. Just by virtue of the fact that you are concentrating so hard on really seeing this picture vividly, you will be focusing a tremendous amount of mental energy, or power, on this subject. Your mind will readily absorb all of these details quickly.

Occasionally repeat these meditations over the next few hours to burn these facts into your mind for a long time. If an idea is to remain in our long-term memory, it will have to be something that we tend to use often, or we have to take time to meditate on it every so often. Usually, we need to review ideas and facts that we want to retain in our long-term memory at least every month.

## CAUSES FOR NOT REMEMBERING NAMES

Not only can we employ this one picture technique with textbook information to learn but also in learning the names of people. Wouldn't you like to be able to attend a party made up predominantly of strangers and be able to know everyone attending by name after meeting them once? Well, you can do just that with the information that I will give you in the rest of this chapter!

There are three primary causes for not remembering a person's name. First of all, a reason for not remembering is that we never heard the name as it was pronounced when we were introduced. It is very important to listen to how the name is pronounced. If you do not hear it, or it was not clear to you, have it repeated. You must hear it and understand how to pronounce it before you can expect to remember it later.

Another cause that hinders our ability to remember a name is that some are not tangible names. They are not the names of things that can be seen in the mind's eye. Most people tend to be eye-minded and need to be able to see the name in their mind.

Now for the third cause of this problem. How many times have you come in contact with someone you know that you have met before because you remember having seen their face but you cannot seem to recall their name? Again, we are eye minded so we automatically recall having seen the face but we cannot recall the name because we did not associate it to the face. So, there you have the three main reasons or causes for not being able to remember a person's name.

## THREE STEPS FOR REMEMBERING NAMES AND FACES

What can be done to eliminate these causes and therefore the problem of not remembering names and faces? The first thing that can be done is to make sure to concentrate on both the name and the face when you meet someone. Secondly, you must make the name picturable if it is not tangible in nature. In other words, you must create an unusual image in your mind that will represent the name. What we need to do then is to develop some systematic steps to help you do all of these things each and every time you meet a new person.

Here are three steps for improving your memory for names and faces. First, we must choose a word for the name that can be pictured. Remember that we tend to be eye-minded. We remember what we can see, even if it is only in our minds. Let us say that we have just met a Mr. Gordon. We must now choose a tangible word that sounds enough like "Gordon" to remind us of this name. Let us use "garden".

This will only aid our memory. Just searching your mind for a suitable word will cause you to concentrate on the name how it is spelled, and how it is pronounced. This takes care of the first cause for forgetting a person's name.

The second step is to select an outstanding feature about this person's face and make a caricature of the person emphasizing this striking feature. This step helps you to concentrate on the face of the individual. While you are looking for a striking feature on this person's face, you will actually be paying close attention to all of his features. You may find such outstanding features as a receding hairline, thick eyebrows, or maybe a peculiar nose.

Let us say that Mr. Gordon, in this case, has very thick eyebrows. This is important! It must be outstanding or striking to you so that the next time you see him this very same feature will stand out for you. Once you have decided on the outstanding feature, you make a caricature of him in your mind' s eye emphasizing this feature.

The third step is to associate the image representing the name with the caricature in an unusual manner. For Mr. Gordon, see him with thick — very thick — eyebrows raking in a garden. The plants in this garden though are not ordinary plants. They are special — unusual! They are three-foot stalks with three-inch eyebrows for flowers.

This garden of these unusual plants extend as far as the eye can see. This should overcome the third cause for not remembering the name that goes with a face. When you see this face again you will also see this caricature and the garden thus reminding you of his name.

I might add that if there are some facts pertaining to the person that you would like to remember, you can create images to represent each of them and include these images in this one picture.

You should now know how to apply this one-picture technique of using associations. We will discuss the second technique in the next chapter.

# 3.

# THE CHAIN METHOD

In addition to the one-picture technique, we have the chain method technique. This technique is very versatile and will probably be employed in most learning situations.

## A CHAIN OF IDEAS

The chain method is used to list ideas in a specific sequence. With this technique you will form a mental image of the first idea and you will then associate it to the image of the next idea on the list to form a mental picture of two images. Adding the next idea, you must associate the last image in your mind to the new image standing for the third idea on the list. You will repeat this through all of the items on your list. When you finish you will have a chain of mental images from left to right. If there are details to be learned concerning these ideas, you should meditate on them as you go over the chain of mental images. Meditation is thinking an idea or subject through. So, when I suggest that you meditate, you will simply be talking to yourself about the ideas and their details. After having formed the chain and having talked over the details with yourself, you are ready to test yourself. You can see what you have learned by now visualizing the chain of images while reciting all you can recall about each idea in turn. You should be able to remember most of the material the first time, depending, of course, on how difficult the material is. Your deep concentration on seeing these mental images vividly will force your mind to absorb all or most of the details that should go along with them.

Perhaps I had better explain here what I mean when I say details. Details are statements or facts that relate in some way to the main idea of which you have now formed a mental image. You will not remember sentences verbatim, but if you will note in your mind as you read and study a key word or phrase for the full statement that you want to learn, you will be able to remember the statement in your own words. This is all that is necessary in most learning situations, even in college. You can, however, learn what needs to be learned verbatim in the same way but with more repetitions of the exact words of the statement.

This technique, as with all of these memory techniques, will enable you to quickly get the information off of the printed page and into your mind. You then can go about doing other things that need to be done. You should take time every so often to mentally review the images again and recite all of the details that you desire to retain. If you realize that you have forgotten something, you can look it up and go over it again in your mind. You will see that this undoubtedly is the fastest way to learn. This will mean a lot to you if you are a college student because a college student seems to always be pressed for time.

## MAGAZINE ARTICLES

Now let us take this knowledge of how to learn a list of things in a specific order and apply it to remembering articles read in a magazine. The first step in reading a magazine article is to discover the subject or theme of it. Once this has been determined you will need to create an image to represent it. Search for a key word that will cause you to recall the subject matter when you see the word again. Remember it has to be a word that can be pictured. Now create this subject image.

Next, locate the first main point. Here you must find a key word which can be pictured also. Create this image and associate the image of the first main point to the subject image. This gives you your first picture. It is a picture of two images related together in some way. In some unique way, I might add.

As you continue reading, locate the second main point in the article. Again, note a key word that can be pictured and that will help you recall that point. As before, create an image and associate it to the image of the first main point. This will form a second picture. When you look at this picture all you will see are the images of the first main idea and the second main idea.

Let us think about what we have done for a moment. It is important that you understand perfectly what I have said. When you think of the subject of the article, the subject image will come to mind along with the image of the first main point that you associated (related to it in some unique way) to it creating the first mental picture. You now know what the first main point of the article is just by thinking of the subject image. Once you see this, the image of the first main point will recall another picture to mind that is similar. This second picture will consist of the image of the first main point and the image of the second main point.

Note that the image for the first main point of the article is in two pictures. This is done so you can associate it one way with the first image and another way with the third image. For instance, let us say that we are reading an article in a business magazine and the subject is how to have a good relationship with your customers. This is not the title of the article, just the theme of it. It is a short article and only has two main points. The first main point in my own words is how to know your customers better. The second main point of the article is how to keep them informed about what your business has to offer them.

For the first image that would represent the theme of the article, I would think of a customer in a relay race. You know, a customer wearing a hat, a white shirt and tie, jogging shorts, and holding out a relay race baton. The first main point could be represented by a large brain (knowledge) with a small body. Now associate these two images together to get the first picture. See the customer who is in the relay actually chasing or racing around the store after the brain man. He is frantically looking around behind himself as he races through the store to get away.

Now you must associate the brain man which was the last thing that you had in your mind with the image of the second main point. The second picture will still have this brain man in it but this image of the brain man must be associated to the image I will now create to stand for the second main point of the article. The second point was about how to keep one's customers informed about what your business has to offer them. The word "informed" will help me recall this point. The image for "informed" will be foam. Putting the two images together, we will have this for a second picture. We will see this brain man drowning in a tremendous mound of foam. The brain man represented the idea of knowing your customers, but it also reminded you that this same image also appeared in another picture. A picture in which this same brain man almost drowns in a mound of foam — inform.

If there were a third main point, the image of foam would be in the third picture associated to the third main point. If you think of one of the images in any one picture you will automatically think of the other image that is in the same picture. Just remember in using the chain method you will always have pictures of two images each. When you see the first picture the second image in it will help you recall the second picture. The second picture contains two images associated together in some unique way. It contains the second image that is in the first picture and a second image which stands for the next point to remember.

So far in these two examples you have two pictures representing symbolically three ideas. You have the subject image and the image for the first main point in the first picture. In the second picture you have the image representing the first main idea repeated and the image for the second main point. When you want to add the third main idea to you chain, form a third picture. This third picture will have the second main point of the article repeated and associated to the image that will represent the third main point of the article. Continue this procedure until all of the main points of the article have been added to the chain of pictures.

At this point you should begin reviewing the mental images of the chain. As you see each image in turn it should remind you of the key word and therefore of the main thought. After going through them once, you can now go back and meditate on the details of each main point. Continue reviewing your mental images and meditating on the details until you are satisfied that you know the material and that you can recall the main points and details quickly and with ease. You may need to do this only a couple of times with fairly easy material. With harder, more difficult material, it may take more times. You must decide what you need to know and how well, but you will be truly amazed at how easily you will be able to learn the information read in a magazine article.

## SUBHEADINGS IN TEXTBOOKS

This technique also lends itself well to learning from a textbook. There will be more information in a chapter in a textbook than in a magazine article. A textbook chapter covers a broader subject area. It usually is divided into main headings that appear in bold print and are further divided into subheadings also appearing in perhaps smaller bold type.

If you feel that you need to learn a subheading and the main points in the paragraphs below it, then handle it as you would an article in a magazine. Think of the subheading as the subject of an article. Search the paragraphs below for the main ideas of the subheading that you want to remember. Then follow the same procedures I just discussed for remembering what was read in a magazine article. The only difference is that you will now be working with all of the main ideas of the subheading located in a few paragraphs instead of being strung out over several pages. Then continue with each other subheading and paragraphs in turn if you feel that it is important enough to learn.

## MAIN HEADINGS AND SUBHEADINGS

Another situation that you might find when studying a textbook is this. You may feel that you need to learn a main heading, all of its subheadings, and the main details under each subheading. This could be the case when you think there may be an essay question asked on an up-coming test that would require you to be able to recall these points or even be able to apply these points to a given situation described to prove that you fully understand them.

The first step in applying the chain method to this situation would be to find a key word which can be pictured and will remind you of the bold printed main heading. Create an image to use for representing this keyword and in turn the thought. This is the subject image.

Secondly, you will need to find a keyword for the first subheading and create an image for it. This will be the first main idea image. Associate this image to the subject image. You now have your first link in the chain.

For the second link of the chain, find a keyword for the second subheading and create an image for it also. Associate this third image to the second image. Continue this procedure until you have a chain of images in the mind representing all of the subheadings under the main heading.

When you have finished this you are now ready to begin reviewing these mental images, thinking of the keywords and the thoughts for which they stand. You will also need to meditate on the details under each subheading. This is the same procedure that we did with the magazine article.

## HELP FOR LEARNING DETAILS

This is the way I recommend that you study details, but I realize that there may come a time when you would need a little more· help with the details. So, for these rare situations I will now give you an alternate way to ensure that you remember the details using this chain method.

First, create an image for each detail under a subheading that you want to add on to your original chain. Go to the image on the original chain that represents this main idea to which these details relate. At this point you will need to duplicate this main idea image so that it is separate from the main or original chain. The reason for this is to avoid confusion. This duplicate will serve as the beginning link of the new branching chain of details related to this particular main idea. This may be an exact duplicate, or it may be the same item but changed to some degree. You can then associate your first detail image to it. Continue by associating the next detail image to this first detail image. Once all of these detail images have been added, you will have developed a branching chain of the details. Be sure that you have completed the original chain of main idea images first. This will ensure that the original chain of images representing the main ideas will stand out in your mind like the trunk of a tree while the chain, or chains, standing for the details will be as branches off from this trunk.

Again, I am giving this idea to you for such rare cases that you feel your natural memory would not be able to recall the details without an aid.

## PREPARING FOR ESSAY EXAMS

Let us look at a situation that a student might find himself in and one in which this use of the chain method would be appropriate. Suppose that you were studying a chapter in a textbook on physical science in preparation for a college exam. In this chapter you found a major heading concerning the Scientific Method. Under this heading were seven subheadings in bold print, each being one of the seven steps of the Scientific Method. These subheadings, along with the accompanying details, covered two or three pages of the text material of this chapter. If you would like, look up the Scientific Method in the index of a science book and see the type of material you would be trying to learn if you were a student with this assignment.

To apply the chain method, we must first relegate each step to a key word or phrase that can be pictured in an unusual manner. Look at exhibit #1 for a list of key words or phrases that I am using to stand for each step of the Scientific Method.

Our next step will be to develop an image for the term "Scientific Method", which is the subject, and an image for each subsequent step of the Scientific Method, which would be the subheadings. The second column in exhibit #1 will show you possible images that would remind us of these key words and hence the steps we want to remember. You may think of other images that you would prefer to use and that is fine. Whatever comes to your mind will be the best image to use, but I am listing these to let you see how I would set up this material for learning it.

## THE SCIENTIFIC METHOD

| Key Words | Images |
|-----------|--------|
| Idea or observation | Eye/binoculars |
| Statement of problem | Skates |
| Hypothesis | Highball or hippopotamus |
| Controlled experiment | Convict stripes on an egg |
| Collect & analyze | Anvil |
| Compare results with hypothesis | Pear opens up like a compact with a mirror |
| Perform further experiments for confirmation | Perfume bottle |

Exhibit #1

We are now ready to make a chain from these images. As we have done before, we will associate the first subheading image to our subject image. We always add images from left to right when working with main idea chains. This is how we maintain a definite order of thoughts. Next, we will associate the second subheading image to the first in an unusual way. We continue in this manner with the rest of the images. When we finish associating all of the images together, we will have a chain from left to right. It will begin with the subject image, then the first subheading image, the second and so on through all seven subheadings.

So far, we have only put the information in skeleton form into our mind. This is much like writing a brief outline on a scrap of paper. To add flesh to this skeletal framework, we must meditate over the headings and their related details. We must read and think about what is stated under each of these points. Looking up from the text periodically to talk over these points and details with ourself using the chain of images to remind us of each subheading is absolutely necessary. As we concentrate on these images and try to picture in our mind what the details are describing or explaining, we will be burning these ideas and relationships to each subheading into our mind.

When I say picture the details, I mean to see in our mind what actually comes to mind normally when we think about something. Here we are not using images as substitutes for our thoughts. We are just consciously visualizing our thoughts so that they will return in the same form when me again review this chain of images.

If you are in school you will find this technique to be a great help in preparing for essay and short answer exams. You will automatically be prepared for objective tests.

## USE WITH ACROSTICS

Finally, the chain method can be used in conjunction with an acrostic. An acrostic is a series of letters in a pattern that is easy to remember. Most of the time it forms a word. The letters of this acrostic represent the initial letter of a key word which in turn will remind you of a thought or main idea that you want to remember. This is used many times by speakers. Sometimes it is only known to themselves to help remember the main points of the speech. At other times the acrostic can be made to form a word that is related to the subject of the speech and the speaker informs his audience so that they can follow it as an outline for his speech. This then becomes an aid to help them remember the main points of his speech.

In using an acrostic to help remember the main points as well as the subordinate points of a speech, the speaker would first make an image of the key word of the thought to be remembered by the first letter of the acrostic. Then he would continue doing this with all of the letters of the acrostic. As the speaker gives his speech, he will take each letter of the acrostic in turn and each one will remind him of the image representing the thought or main idea at this point of the speech. These images will be the first links of separate chains to be developed concerning each of these main speech ideas and their subordinate points.

To form the first chain that will include the first main idea and its subordinate points, determine each subordinate thought and reduce it to a key word that can be pictured. Make an image of each that will remind you of the thought. Now associate the image of the first subordinate point to the image of the first idea. Then proceed to associate the image of the second subordinate point to the image of the first subordinate idea. Continue until all subordinate points are included in the first chain. At this point you will repeat this second letter of the acrostic. Do this with all letters of your acrostic and you will have an outline of the main and subordinate ideas of your speech in your mind.

As you deliver your speech you will think of your acrostic. The first letter will remind you of the first main thought. Simultaneously, you will also be reminded of the image of the first main idea. This image is associated in some unusual way to the next image which represents the first subordinate idea. This image in turn brings you to the next and so on through the first chain of images.

After going through that chain of images, you will proceed to the next letter of the acrostic. Here you will begin the second chain. Continue until all of the images have been exhausted and your speech will be over.

Unless you are a professional speaker, I would caution you not to use this if called upon to give a speech. With the tension and excitement of giving a speech, your mind could go blank. Leave this to one who is accustomed to delivering speeches. You can, however, use this to practice your speech over and over in your mind before actually giving it. This will help you learn your speech thoroughly. It would be good to use some notes or at least cue words when actually delivering your speech. By practicing in this manner, you may be able to reduce the number of notes you would require to deliver a good speech.

As you can see the chain method can be used in many situations, and it can be employed in many different ways. Be creative! Strive to find new ways in which you can utilize this method to help you learn and remember what needs to be learned.

# 4.

# THE PEG WORD METHOD

In the previous chapter I showed you how to learn ideas in a sequence when order was important. The peg system technique should be used when you need random access to the information stored in your memory. In this chapter I will explain this amazing system and show you how you can put it to use.

## THE PEG SYSTEM

As you know numbers are abstract. Remember when you were dealing with abstract names, we said that we needed a system in which we could picture these names? Well, now we need a system in which we can picture numbers. The system that has been invented uses a phonetic alphabet with assigned numerical values. In other words, the sounds made by certain letters stand for numbers. See exhibit #2 for a table of sounds and the letters that may be employed to produce these sounds.

### Phonetic Alphabet

| 1 | 2 | 3 | 4 | 5 | 6 | 7 | 8 | 9 | 0 |
|---|---|---|---|---|---|---|---|---|---|
| t | n | m | r | l | j | k | f | p | s |
| d | d | | | | ch | hard c | v | b | z |
| | | | | | sh | hard g | ph | | soft c |
| | | | | | soft g | | | | |

Exhibit # 2

This table of sounds is the basis for the peg word system. I will now also give you a list of 100 peg words (see exhibit #3). These peg words are in a certain sequence. Each word stands for the number out to the side of it. Compare the letters with those of the table in exhibit #2 and you will see why.

From these 100 words, you can make up any number instantly after you have learned them. Just make a chain of these peg words to form a long number.

They also can be used like hooks on which to hang ideas so that the ideas will be in a numerical sequence and can be retrieved by the number at any time.

## 100 Peg Words

| | | | | | |
|---|---|---|---|---|---|
| | dew | 21 net | 41 rat | 61 chute | 81 fat |
| 2 | knee | 22 nun | 42 run | 62 chin | 82 fan |
| 3 | May | 23 name | 43 ram | 63 chime | 83 foam |
| 4 | oar | 24 Nero | 44 roar | 64 jar | 84 fur |
| 5 | owl | 25 nail | 45 rail | 65 jello | 85 full |
| 6 | chew | 26 niche | 46 rash | 66 judge | 86 fish |
| 7 | key | 27 neck | 47 rack | 67 jack | 87 fake |
| 8 | fee | 28 knife | 48 roof | 68 chief | 88 fife |
| 9 | bow | 29 knob | 49 rope | 69 chip | 89 fob |
| 10 | toes | 30 moose | 50 lace | 70 case | 90 base |
| 11 | tot | 31 mat | 51 lot | 71 cat | 91 bat |
| 12 | tin | 32 man | 52 line | 72 can | 92 ban |
| 13 | time | 33 mummy | 53 lime | 73 cam | 93 bum |
| 14 | tar | 34 mare | 54 lure | 74 car | 94 bear |
| 15 | tail | 35 mail | 55 lily | 75 coal | 95 bell |
| 16 | dish | 36 match | 56 latch | 76 cash | 96 batch |
| 17 | tack | 37 mack | 57 lock | 77 coke | 97 back |
| 18 | tough | 38 movie | 58 loft | 78 cuff | 98 beef |
| 19 | top | 39 mop | 59 lobe | 79 cap | 99 beep |
| 20 | nose | 40 rose | 60 cheese | 80 vase | 100 daises |

## Exhibit #3

Also, I must mention that there are some principles that must be followed to avoid confusion. Remember that it is the sound made by letters that indicate the number and never the letter. Therefore, it is obvious that a silent letter in a word will not be counted as a number. No vowels will be used to represent numbers and all double letters will only count as one number represented by that sound.

## TEXTBOOK CHAPTER

Now that we have explained the peg system, let us begin applying it to specific learning situations and assignments. We will first explain how to use this system to learn information in a textbook chapter. After reading the chapter, begin with the first bold heading that you see is important and has some main ideas and details related to it that you feel you should learn. You do not have to work with every bold heading unless you are trying to develop an outline of the chapter in your mind. Remember that the best principle is to learn what is important, not every little thing that the chapter mentions.

Looking at the first important bold heading, determine a key word or phrase that can stand for this heading. Remember it must be picturable. Now create an image to represent it. Next associate this image to the image of the first peg word. If you are using the peg word list above, the image of the first heading would be associated to the word dew. The image of the second heading would be associated to the picture or image of the second peg word in the list above which is knee. Do this to all of the bold headings that you feel are important and then go back to work with the main points of each. I will give you other peg lists that can also be used for this kind of learning situation.

Under each bold heading you will need to determine what are the main points that will be needed to be remembered. Once you have located them decide on a key word or phrase that can be pictured or symbolized for each. Then create the image that will represent each main idea. After this is done make a chain of these images representing the main ideas. Next, the first link of the chain should be connected to the image already associated to the image of the peg word. Continue with each peg word and main points until all have been completed.

Now all that remains is to handle the details related to these main ideas. Go over the peg words and chains of main points in your mind while looking the reading material over for any important details. When you discover details that you feel are important, you simply meditate on them and visualize how they relate to each main point. You will be amazed how easily these details will fall into place while concentrating so hard on these main point images.

Once you have finished using this or any of the following peg lists, you must clear each peg word picture so you will no longer hold the association between it and the item you have been associating with it. This is necessary in order to use each peg word picture again. You want to be able to associate something entirely different with it next time. You will accomplish this by simply picturing each peg word picture, which now has another picture associated with it, without that picture or item associated with it any longer. You now only see the peg word pictures. They no longer help you recall any particular idea or picture. A Peg word list is used similarly to a blackboard. You will note certain ideas on it temporarily to help in recalling other information. Once you have learned the information you will no longer need the help of the peg word list.

## PER PAGE

I would now like to briefly mention an idea that may come in useful to you in a given situation, especially if you happen to be a teacher or a student. By using the peg words to represent the page numbers of a book, booklet, or magazine article, you can know the page on which a particular subject is located or begins.

Also, you could learn an outline of what is on every page. Sometimes just the knowledge that this can be done will be helpful to you in a specific situation, particularly in school. You may need to learn the outline of several pages in your text for a test that is designed to test you in a little different fashion than most test are designed to do.

Let me go through the steps now that you would need to perform if you were to use this technique in either of these two ways. If you need to know the page on which to locate a particular subject, you would first create a subject image as we have done before. Then associate this image to the appropriate peg word image that stands for the same number as the page you want to remember. When you think of the subject you will see this association and will remember the proper page on which it will be found.

The second way that I mentioned of using this technique was to learn a short outline of ideas on certain numbered pages. To do this simply create an image for each main point on a page. Then make a chain of these main point images that appear on a particular numbered page and associate the first link image to the peg word image for that page number. Finally, meditate on the details that would be related to these main ideas.

This per page idea would only be good to use with a magazine article or a chapter in textbook since only a few peg words would be required. A book would require several hundred peg words. Even though this idea, or technique, may be rarely employed, I did want you to know about it. Who knows, it just may come in handy for you one day.

## PER PARAGRAPH

The next technique I wish to discuss will be most helpful to businessmen whether they be executives, managers, or in middle or entry level positions. This technique enables one to remember subjects and subpoints by the paragraph. This will be especially helpful in learning business procedures according to a procedure's manual.

Business manuals are written in this fashion. Each heading is numbered. The first heading is numbered 1.0, the second would be 2.0, the third would be 3.0 and so on through the entire manual.

Each paragraph that begins a subpoint will also be numbered. The subpoints are numbered 1.1, 1.2, and so on for all subpoints falling under the first heading. The second heading numbered 2.0 will have its first subpoint numbered 2.1, its second 2.2, the third 2.3, and so on. This is helpful in finding the procedures required pertaining to different subject areas.

The peg system can be helpful here by allowing you to remember where different information is located without having to look it up every time it is needed. If you are a business person you will not mind consulting the manual when in doubt about how something is supposed to be done since you know right where to find it. As a result, you will probably become one of the best-informed employees in the office concerning the proper procedures to be used. You do not have to learn all of the details, just know where the heading or subpoint dealing with the point in question is located. You will then be able to read about the details.

I might mention also that there can be other uses for this technique. You may find it helpful to use with written or printed material of yours. Simply number headings and paragraphs as a procedure's manual would be numbered before applying the steps, I am about to tell you. For example, you could be invited to a business meeting to discuss some printed reports or some other printed matter. Different subjects could be raised in regard to these possibly lengthy reports. If you had prepared using this technique for areas that you thought would be possible discussion topics, you would be able to quickly refer to the appropriate sections of the report when needed. You may need to refer to a section to support one of the points that you might be making before the group at sometime during the meeting.

Here is how to learn this material by applying this technique. If you are working with a procedure's manual, the headings and subpoints are already numbered, so create an image for each heading, which will probably be noted with bold typing, that you feel is important and that you want to remember. Use the peg word that represents 10 for 1.0. Associate the image of the bold heading to this peg word. The second bold heading will be associated to the peg word for 20. It will then stand for 2.0.

Next, create an image for each paragraph subject. These will be the subpoints of the bold heading subject matter. Associate the image of the subject matter of the first paragraph to the peg word that represents 11. Eleven will stand for 1.1. The second paragraph image will be associated to the peg word for twelve, standing for 1.2.

For details you can just read about them when you look up these subjects that are listed on your pegs, or you can develop a chain of images to remind you of them and have the first link associated to the appropriate paragraph image.

Another way to handle the details would be to meditate on those that you think you need to know as you concentrate on the image for the related paragraph subject.

## THE SPREAD SHEET

This next memory technique will be of great value to teachers and students and anyone who needs to learn information from tables, charts, and maps. This technique can even be utilized to remember the outline of a book. I call it the spread sheet because it is like a computer spread sheet program.

We will use our one hundred peg words for this technique with a little change. Since you will always know these one hundred peg words it will be easy to set up when it is needed. The object is to arrange the list of one hundred peg words so that they will form ten columns of ten peg words. To do this make ten columns of these peg words in this manner. The first column will begin with the peg word for eleven. This will be followed by the peg word for twelve right below it. Continue this column down to the peg word for nineteen. After the peg word for nineteen will come the peg word for ten.

The second column will be done similarly to this. Begin with the peg word for twenty-one, then follow below it with the peg word for twenty-two, twenty-three and so on through twenty-nine. End the column with the peg word for twenty.

Continue writing the columns like this through the peg word for ninety-nine. At this point we will use a peg list of ten numbers from one to nine and ending with a peg word for zero. These peg words, however, will not be the ones in the regular list of one hundred peg words. This column will be made up of ten peg words which all start with an "h", the first letter of the word "hundred". In other words, your last column will begin with the peg word for one, "hat" followed by the peg word for two, "hen" and on down through the peg word for nine, "hub". This column will end with the peg word for zero that begins with an "h", "hose".

See exhibit #4.

## Spread Sheet

| tot | net | mat | rat | lot | chute | cat | fat | bat | hat |
|-----|-----|-----|-----|-----|-------|-----|-----|-----|-----|
| tin | nun | man | run | line | chin | can | fan | ban | hen |
| time | name | mummy | ram | lime | chime | cam | foam | bum | home |
| tar | nero | mare | roar | lure | jar | car | fur | bear | hare |
| tail | nail | mail | rail | lilly | jello | coal | full | bell | hail |
| dish | niche | match | rash | latch | judge | cash | fish | batch | hash |
| tac | neck | mack | rack | lock | jack | coke | fake | back | hike |

| tough | knife | movie | roof | loft | chief | cuff | fife | beef | hoof |
| top | knob | mop | rope | lobe | chip | cap | fob | beep | hub |
| toes | nose | moose | rose | lace | cheese | case | vase | base | hose |

Exhibit #4

You now have a spread sheet of one hundred memory positions. Each position can be referred to by its coordinates. For instance, the first block or cell would be referred to as 1,1. This would be column 1, row 1. Always refer to the column first. The last position in the table would be in the tenth column and the tenth row. This would be represented by the word "hose". To refer to it by its coordinates, you would say: 10,10. The cell in the sixth column on the fourth row would be 6,4. If the peg word for 64 were "jar" then you would remember the item to be placed in this cell by associating the image of this item to your image for "jar". You could even place a number of items in an individual cell by beginning the association with your image for "jar ' and then a chain of images representing all of the other items to be remembered. Exhibit #5 shows how each position can be referred to by a column and row number designation.

This is probably all that you will need, but there may arise an occasion in which you will need to label columns. You could, of course, use the cells on the first row for remembering the column labels, but there is a way to label your columns and still retain 100 memory positions for your data.

To do this will require that you learn ten additional peg words which will stand for the letter's "A" through -"J". See the peg words for these in exhibit #6. Rather than just giving you the ten words needed for this situation, I will give you the peg words for all of the letters in the alphabet.

| 1 | 11 | 21 | 31 | 41 | 51 | 61 | 71 | 81 | 91 | 101 |
|----|----|----|----|----|----|----|----|----|----|-----|
| 2 | 12 | 22 | 32 | 42 | 52 | 62 | 72 | 82 | 92 | 102 |
| 3 | 13 | 23 | 33 | 43 | 53 | 63 | 73 | 83 | 93 | 103 |
| 4 | 14 | 24 | 34 | 44 | 54 | 64 | 74 | 84 | 94 | 104 |
| 5 | 15 | 25 | 35 | 45 | 55 | 65 | 75 | 85 | 95 | 105 |
| 6 | 16 | 26 | 36 | 46 | 56 | 66 | 76 | 86 | 96 | 106 |
| 7 | 17 | 27 | 37 | 47 | 57 | 67 | 77 | 87 | 97 | 107 |
| 8 | 18 | 28 | 38 | 47 | 58 | 68 | 78 | 88 | 98 | 108 |
| 9 | 19 | 29 | 39 | 49 | 59 | 69 | 79 | 89 | 99 | 109 |
| 10 | 10 | 20 | 30 | 40 | 50 | 60 | 70 | 80 | 90 | 100 |

Exhibit #5

## Alphabet words

| | | | | |
|---|---|---|---|---|
| A — ape | F — elf | K — cake | P — pea | V — veal |
| B — Bee | G — jeans | L — el | Q — cue | W — double-bubble |
| C — Seal | H — ale | M — ham | R — hour | X — eggs |
| D — deal | I — eye | N — end | S — hiss | Y — YMCA |
| E — Easel | J — jail | O — cherrio | T — tea | Z — Zebra |
| | | | U — ewe | |

Exhibit #6

Now label each column with a letter of the alphabet beginning with the column with the peg word for eleven at the top. This will be labeled "A". The next column that begins with the peg word for twenty-one will be labeled "B" and so on through "J". "J" will be the label for the column beginning with the peg word for one that begins with an "h".

Finally, number from one to nine down he left side of this table beginning at the peg word for eleven and continuing down to the peg word for nineteen. The last row will be labeled ten so place a ten out to the left of the peg word "toes" which is the last peg word in column one. When all of this is finished your table should look like

|    | A  | B  | C  | D  | E  | F  | G  | H  | I  | J |
|----|----|----|----|----|----|----|----|----|----|---|
| 1  | 11 | 21 | 31 | 41 | 51 | 61 | 71 | 81 | 91 | 1 |
| 2  | 12 | 22 | 32 | 42 | 52 | 62 | 72 | 82 | 92 | 2 |
| 3  | 13 | 23 | 33 | 43 | 53 | 63 | 73 | 83 | 93 | 3 |
| 4  | 14 | 24 | 34 | 44 | 54 | 64 | 74 | 84 | 94 | 4 |
| 5  | 15 | 25 | 35 | 45 | 55 | 65 | 75 | 85 | 95 | 5 |
| 6  | 16 | 26 | 36 | 46 | 56 | 66 | 76 | 86 | 96 | 6 |
| 7  | 17 | 27 | 37 | 47 | 57 | 67 | 77 | 87 | 97 | 7 |
| 8  | 18 | 28 | 38 | 47 | 58 | 68 | 78 | 88 | 98 | 8 |
| 9  | 19 | 29 | 39 | 49 | 59 | 69 | 79 | 89 | 99 | 9 |
| 10 | 10 | 20 | 30 | 40 | 50 | 60 | 70 | 80 | 90 | 0 |

Exhibit #7

You do not have to write out all of this to use it. I just wanted to take you through the setting up of this arrangement step by step so you would completely understand it and its purpose. What we have accomplished is that now we have a notation system. Chess can be played by mail using a notation system that indicates every single square on the chessboard which has a total of sixty-four. This is the same idea but expanded to include one hundred positions and can be used in a variety of ways.

One of the ways that this technique could be used would be for learning the outline of a book. Make an image to stand for the title of each chapter and associate it to the peg words that represent "A", "B", "C", and the other letters through "J", which are for the purpose of labeling each column of information. The peg words under each of these can be associated to the main points in the chapter once you create an image to represent them.

Another use of this spread sheet technique would be for learning geographical territories such as nations, states, cities, etc. In your mind merely superimpose this grid over whatever map you are using. In other words, in your mind this map would be divided into columns like this grid. Make images to stand for the geographical territories you are studying and associate them to the peg word that would be closest to its actual location on the map if this grid were superimposed over it.

Let us suppose that you needed to learn information from a chart. Perhaps you may be expected to basically reproduce the chart of information on a test, if you are a student. Imagine that this spread sheet is superimposed over this chart and mentally divide the chart into areas or columns. Note which peg word or words would be in these areas. Develop images for each piece of information that you need to remember and associate them to the images of the peg words which are located in the same areas.

I think you will find many uses for this technique. With this technique you will be able to refer to specific bits of information by letter and number. For instance, you will be able to know what information is located at, say "G,5". You know that "G" is the seventh letter of the alphabet so the information will be in the column beginning with "71". Your information will be associated to the number "75". Remember that the peg word for "G" is only used as a label for that column, a title for that column of items or information.

## THE HOUSE OUTLINE

Here is another way to remember a short outline using peg words. This peg word list consists of objects in a house. Used properly one can remember an outline of five headings, and as many as five main points made about each of the five headings, and a number of subpoints about each of the main points.

What I have done is to list items that are normally found in the various rooms of one's home. You may use the list I will give you are you may try to develop a similar list from the objects you will find in your own home. It would probably be easier for you to remember objects that are in your own home.

I chose five rooms in my house for this list. It is important to use the rooms in the order in which they would come as you would walk through the house. Of course, some would be across the hall from another, so simply think of walking through the house stopping at the rooms on the right before stopping at the rooms across on the left. I started with my den, then the bathroom, then I crossed over to the left side of the hall to my son's bedroom, then the living room, and finally the kitchen. This would make a full tour of my house if I were to walk through it. I skipped two bedrooms in the tour. That is because if you think about it, all bedrooms have very similar objects. This would be confusing.

The first thing that I have done with my list is to establish a particular object for each of these rooms to be used with a heading. For instance, the den is the first room on my tour and is therefore representing Roman numeral one on my outline. The object that I will first think of in this room will be the China cabinet. Once I determine the first heading of an article, I will create an image that will stand for it. I will then associate this heading image to the China cabinet to remember that this heading is the first heading on my outline. I will create an image for each subsequent heading in the article. Then I will associate each of these to the object designated in each room to represent the second, third, fourth, and fifth Roman numeral points on the outline.

Let me list the rooms for you now along with their respective object standing for its ranking order indicated on an outline by the Roman numerals from I - V.

|      |              |               |
|------|--------------|---------------|
| I.   | Den          | China cabinet |
| II.  | Bathroom     | shower        |
| III. | Son's bedroom | mirror       |
| IV.  | Living room  | open closet   |
| V.   | Kitchen      | counter       |

Now for the individual sub-point peg words pictured by specific objects within each of these designated rooms. First on our tour through the house is the den. I have already mentioned that the piece of furniture in the den that represents Roman numeral I is the China cabinet. So, associate the first main point image to the China cabinet.

Let us look at the various objects in these rooms that can be made to be useful in remembering an outline. Each of the following objects or pieces of furniture will represent "A" through "E" of an outline. The first object standing for "A" is a floor lamp. It resembles the numeral 1. The second object is a rocking chair. It resembles the numeral two. "B" is the second letter of the alphabet and should be assigned to the second sub-point of an outline. The sofa will represent the "C" since it has three cushions. The dining table has four legs and will therefore represent the fourth letter of the alphabet, "D". The "E" or fifth letter designating a sub-point in an outline will be the Television. The television is five because it has a channel five test pattern on its screen momentarily. This then is the first room on our tour of the house, and also gives us six hooks for storing information. One hook or peg for the main point of the article that you are reading and five hooks or pegs for the sub-points.

Our second section of the outline will begin in the bathroom. I first think of the shower head to represent the second Roman numeral. "A" will be represented by a towel that hangs over a towel bar. It hangs like a "1". The "B" will be assigned to the commode. It, like a chair, resembles to some extent a "2". The three water faucets in the tub will remind us of the "C' in our outline. For the "D" which is the fourth letter of the alphabet, we will use the linen closet with its four shelves. Finally, a small candle with fire on it will remind you of five or the fifth letter of the alphabet which is the "E". There you have the hooks or pegs for the second main point and its five sub-point pegs.

Coming to my son's room, our third room and third main point of the outline, we think of the mirror. Close by the mirror is my son's clock radio with the time set at one o'clock. I think you know why. The second sub-point will be represented by the two windows. Two windows for the second sub-point. Now we need an object that will remind us of three and the third letter of the alphabet, "C". There is no such object in this room so I will invent one. My son does have a stool. Even though it is a four-legged stool I will picture it in my mind as a three-legged stool for my purposes. Our fourth object will be his bed. It has four posts and therefore reminds me of four and four in turn reminds me of "D", the fourth letter of the alphabet. Again, we will improvise for an object to represent "5" or the letter "E". My son has a brief case. I will picture a hand with five fingers holding the handle of this brief case. You see how easy it is to force things to fit our purposes?

Our fourth Roman numeral and its five sub-point peg words will be discussed next. The fourth room on our tour of the house will be the living room. We will use the closet to represent the fourth Roman numeral and main point of our outline. Just picture the image substitute for the fourth main point idea of your outline in the closet in some unique way. See the two images together and you have associated them to each other. For the first sub-point under the fourth main point heading, we will picture a grand piano. It has only one lid which has been prompted open which should reinforce the idea that the piano stands for one or the first sub-point. Next will be the stereo (referring to two) set with two earphones to remind us that this peg word is the second subpoint under the fourth main point. For the third point see with me a picture on the wall with the three bears and Goldilocks in it. The three bears to help us recall that this is the third sub-point of the outline. The fourth sub-point peg word will be the coffee table with four table legs. Finally, the fifth object will be the book case with five book shelves.

Our final room is the kitchen. I think of the counter as representing the fifth Roman numeral of the mental outline. The image that I would use to substitute for the fifth main idea of a magazine article or the chapter of a book would be placed mentally on this counter top in some unique way. The first sub-point will be represented by the washer. The washer comes first in the kitchen and it only has one lid. The second sub-point will be represented by the refrigerator. It is easy to remember because it has two doors. Thirdly, we have the sink. Now here again I use my imagination. I only have a double sink, but I need it to represent three. In order to do this, I picture the sink in my house to be a triple sink. This simply makes it easier to remember it as the third point. Our stove comes next and it has four eyes on it. This will remind us that this stove represents the fourth sub-point on the outline. The final sub-point will be represented by a plastic kitchen trash can. To remember that this item is the fifth, we could picture it with an ivy design on it. Ivy sounds like "five".

This is a quick outline peg system that will enable you to learn an outline quickly of what you have read or the information that you are studying. Practice with it and you will see how practical it is.

## THE "D" LIST

Now let us look at another technique that will be very useful to you every single day. It is best to reserve these 100 words for use with numerical data like long numbers and dates. It would be well to develop other shorter peg word lists to use as hooks to which you can attach other data.

For instance, you can develop a specialized peg word list to help you outline what needs to be accomplished each day of the week. Since there are only seven days in the week, you will only need seven peg words. Let us make up seven words that begin with the letter "D". This helps us remember that when we want to remember the tasks that we need to perform on a particular day of the week, we need to visualize a particular word on our "D" list. "D" is for day. Now each of these words must end with a sound that will represent a number from one to seven. The first word, therefore, would begin with a "D" and end with a "D" or "T" to give us the sound for one. This word will represent Sunday, the first day of the week. We will continue this list on through Saturday, the seventh day of the week. The words that I have chosen are these: dead, den, dime, deer, dill, dash, and dock.

Let me give you an idea of how I picture these words. You can, of course, change any of these words according to the principles I have just explained above if another word would be easier for you to picture.

I would represent "dead" by a tombstone. That is something that is easily pictured. The word "den" may be a little harder. Here is what I picture. I picture the fireplace and hearth in my den. The third word, "dime", is represented by an angel with small wings on his head like the one that appears on a dime. I am sure that you have seen mounted deer heads on a wall. That is what I see to represent the word "deer". "Dill" is simple enough. Simply use a large dill pickle in your association. The dashboard of your car can be pictured to represent "dash". Finally, "dock" is pictured as a dock where boats tie up. There you have it. This is a simple way to picture each day of the week in your mind symbolically.

The way to use this "D" list is to sit down at night and plan tomorrow. Think about what needs to be done in your personal life; we will get to what needs to be done on your job in the next section. A pocket calendar is also helpful. Look at what may be listed on it for tomorrow and make images to represent those things. Now glance at the rest of the week and once or twice a week be sure to look beyond this week to keep aware of what will be corning up. Once you have thought up images and associated them together in a chain beginning with the peg word which represents tomorrow, you will be all set when tomorrow morning comes. There will be no stalling around wondering what to do.

The important thing is to remember to use only one peg word at a time. In other words, you make only one mental chain each evening. This chain will be for tomorrow. When tomorrow comes go over the list after each hour at least to see if there is anything that needs to be done. If you think of something else that you need to do today, make an image and add it to the end of the chain. Only add things to the chain; do not remove the things from the chain as you do them. This will only cause confusion and besides you will want to be able to go through this chain in the evening and see how well you did. You should have a good feeling of accomplishment seeing all of the various things that you needed to do that day and that, in fact, you did accomplish all, or most of them.

If you think of something that needs to be done tomorrow, or at some later date, simply jot it down on your pocket calendar. If it is to be done tomorrow you know that you will see it in your calendar this evening when you make up tomorrow's mental outline.

After you use this idea for a while, you will realize that on certain days of the week you may have a particular task to do every week; or you may find that you have a meeting to attend once a month, but always on the same day of the week. How do you avoid confusion?

Let us say, for instance, that Mondays and Thursdays are always the days when our garbage is picked up. What if you always associated garbage to the peg word for Thursday. After a while you will be associating other tasks, or appointments, to the image for garbage rather than the peg word for Thursday. This will cause confusion so here it how to avoid it. Normally begin a chain from left to right. Always attach the first link mentally on the right of the peg word for that day.

When you have a routine task and will be using the same image for it week after week, place it on the left of the peg word.

Here is how I would remember to take the garbage out on Thursdays with the peg word for Thursday being "dill". My image for garbage would be a galvanized garbage can. It has arms and hands and is choking the dill pickle. I might add that eventually you will habitually think about "garbage" when you think about "dill". When that becomes the case, you may leave this "garbage" image off because it is no longer needed to remind you. You will remember to take the garbage out. Of course, you may like to just leave it in and take no chances. Either way is fine and should be strictly up to your preference.

If you wanted to remember to cut the grass, say on Tuesday when you returned home from work, you could picture an extra-large dime mowing the grass. If I had to get off work and go to a dental appointment at 10:00 A.M., I would see the lawn mower cutting and chomping at a large tooth which has a fearful look on its face as it tries to stay out of reach. I would continue with other images for other tasks to be performed, or appointments to be kept. All these will be extending out to the right from the extra-large dime.

This idea of preparing a mental outline of what you need to do each day helps avoid procrastination also. Once you make the outline, you will feel committed to doing whatever is listed on it. It is as if you had written it down. In effect, you did write it down in your mind. You will want to be able to check off each task at the end of the day. This will give you a feeling of having had a very successful day. If by chance you were unable to get around to accomplishing one or more items of a long outline, you will have to add it to tomorrow's outline when you begin preparing it.

This is one of the most important techniques in this book! Use it every day! Also let us mention here that in using peg list words, you clear them once you are finished using them.

This is to say, when you no longer have a use for remembering what to do on, say Wednesday, visualize the peg word for Wednesday with no associations attached. This will erase the information that you temporarily placed on that peg word. It is as easy as erasing a blackboard. Remember that information is to be placed on peg words only for a temporary period of time. It is an aid for getting the information into your mind quickly so you can recall it over a short period of time until you actually learn it or decide that you no longer need this information, as is the case with these lists of things to do each day. You only need these lists for each day and no longer.

## THE "W" LIST

Now that I have shown you how to develop and use a special peg list for outlining your personal life, let me also show you how this same technique can be modified to help you with your job.

It is important to be able to remember the various tasks that you need to perform on your job each day. To help you with this, we can develop another peg word list that will be reserved only for remembering what must be done concerning your job.

For this specialized peg word list, let us make up one that begins with the letter "W", which will stand for work. This list will contain ten peg words. As with the "D" list, all ten of these words will begin with a "W", which has no numerical value; and they will contain only one other consonant, which will have a numerical value of one to ten. The first word will, of course, end with either a "D" or a "T". The second will have to end with a "N" and so on according to our phonetic table. I am supplying you with a list of "W" words that can be used. You will note that the tenth peg word has an "S" for the only other consonant besides the "W". You will know that this stands for ten. If you would like to, you can develop another word that will contain a "W" at the beginning and two consonants in the order that will form the value ten. I prefer to use the "S" sound only. See the list in exhibit #8.

### "W" Pegs

| Wet | Wham | Wheel | Wick | Web |
| Win | Wire | Wash | Wave | Wise |

Exhibit #8

We will use this list differently than we did our "D" list. With the "W" list all ten words can be used for one particular day. In other words, these peg words are hooks that can be used every day to remember up to ten different major tasks by creating an image for each task and associating it to a peg word. Actually, you can remember more than ten tasks by chaining other images to the one already associated to the first "W" word and the second etc. If you have an eleventh task to do on a given day just add its image to the first image already associated to the first "W" peg word. This can be continued on down the rest of the peg words. I think that you will find that you will rarely have more than ten tasks to handle on one work day.

Remember to review this list mentally frequently throughout the day so that you will do what needs to be done and that you will do those things that need to be done at a certain time on time. Again, you should not be concerned about the order of these tasks as you place them on these mental hooks. When you review the list periodically you will know which task needs to be worked on next.

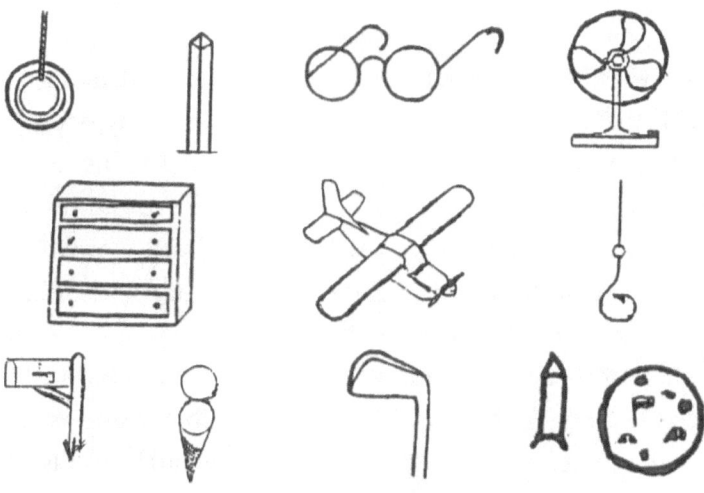

Exhibit #9

## PICTURE PEGS

An additional peg list that I would like to give you is called a picture peg list. Picture pegs look like the number that they symbolize or have several like parts that equal the number that they represent. When you see the picture peg item to will instantly know what number it equals. In exhibit #9 you will see eleven pictures. We have pictures standing for one through ten for you on which to hook things that you need to remember. The picture representing the zero is for labeling your list, if you feel that it is necessary. It is necessary to label your peg list when you are using several of your peg lists to remember different blocks of information and facts about some subject area so you will not get confused.

## PHONETIC PEGS

Along with these special peg word lists, I would like to give you one final list of ten peg words that can be used for any occasion when you need to quickly learn some items or ideas. This list is called the phonetic peg list because instead of using the rules for numerical values that I gave you in the table you will be using peg words that sound like the number itself. A list of these will be found in exhibit #10. As you pronounce each one, you will be reminded of a number from one to ten. Each of these numbers can also be pictured. So, to use this list simple create an image for the idea to be remembered and associate this image to the image of the first peg word. A "wand" sounds like "one" so you will know that this is the first idea on your mental list. This list will be very helpful in many situations. Here in exhibit #10 is the list of phonetic peg words with the accompanying word "zebra" which sounds like zero to be used for labeling the items in some category when you are employing several lists.

### Phonetic Pegs

zebra

| wand | free | dive | seven-up | pine |
| glue | floor | sick | ate | tent |

Exhibit #10

In this chapter we have given an in-depth study into how you can utilize many different kinds of peg words to remember what you need to remember. We even taught you how to use the chain method in conjunction with peg word lists. From these chapters on the subject of memory, you should be able to handle just about any memory problem. Now we need to take a look at the problem of absentmindedness in our next chapter and how we can learn to avoid it.

# 5.

# FORGETTING ABSENTMINDEDNESS

In this chapter I would like to discuss a problem that we all have to face. This problem can be avoided when we understand the proper reason for it. Many people, however, erroneously associate absentmindedness with a problem of memory ability. This is not true. The root of the problem really has to do with the thinking process. We will now show you how to apply four simple principles to avoid the problem of absentmindedness.

The problem of absentmindedness usually has to do with forgetting to do something that should have been done. Also, the person may be so accustomed to doing a particular activity that he later does not recall whether he did it this time or not. By concentrating on the thinking process, we can eliminate both of these situations.

## FOUR PRINCIPLES

To do this, you must see that every task can be broken down into a number of separate steps. Determine the point in the progression of steps that you can often forget to perform or later cannot recall having performed. This is the first principle.

The second principle is to get in the habit of thinking at this point about the step to be performed. Before you start it, check to see if it, in fact, does need to be done. Sometimes this step may not be warranted. Above all, do not get in the habit of automatically doing something. This is why you cannot remember later whether you did a particular step or not. You have done it habitually for so long that it requires no concentrated thinking on your part anymore.

The third step that you must take is to make sure that the step is performed and not forgotten. It may be necessary to build into the progression of steps a memory aid to make you think about doing it at the right time, but we will explain this later in our examples.

And now for the all-important fourth step. This will prevent you from later wondering if you accomplished the task or not. You must pause and picture the step having been performed.

## I FORGOT IT AGAIN

Let us give you a couple of examples to demonstrate how to apply these principles. Our first example is a very simple problem that I am sure many men face from time to time. What happens when you feel a sneeze coming on? You immediately remember your handkerchief, don't you? But sometimes you find that you did not remember it when you were dressing earlier that morning. How can you be sure to remember to put your handkerchief in your pocket every morning? The answer is to apply these principles that combat absentmindedness.

The first step calls for you to devise a certain order of steps for dressing. In this case let us use the following order: (1) step into your pants;   (2) button them; (3) zip them; (4) put on your belt; (5) put your handkerchief in a pocket and whatever else goes in the other pockets.

The second step will call for you to think about what you are doing while dressing. Think about dressing in this particular order which you have determined would be best.

The third step is to make sure that we put the handkerchief in your pocket. To make sure you should use a memory aid. Here is what you do to remember to do it each and every time you dress. When you put your belt on, don't buckle it at first. Allow the unbuckled belt to remind you that the handkerchief step needs to now be performed. Put your handkerchief in your pocket and buckle your belt. You would not forget that! Then continue dressing.

## DID I OR DIDN'T I

In this example above step four was not required but to be sure that you have an appreciation for it when it is needed, I would like to give you another example. These are very simple, common situations, but they explain the points that you need to know. You will be able to apply these principles to more complex circumstances at work or around your home. So, get a thorough understanding of these two examples!

Think about this! You have left home in a hurry on the way to work. This morning you got up unusually early so you could go in to the office early and catch up on some work. Rather than disturb your wife, you prepared a quick breakfast for yourself. About halfway to work you begin to wonder if in your haste you might have forgotten to turn off the stove. Fortunately, in this case you could call your wife and have her check, but had she not been home you would probably have had to return home to be sure. This type of absentmindedness can cause a lot of unnecessary worry and loss of valuable time. Why not learn to apply these four principles and avoid them for good!

As before in applying these principles, the first one calls for deciding on a specific order of steps for the task. Let us make these steps as simple as possible. No matter how complex a task maybe you can do your best to simplify it here. This should be the order: (1) food on or in the stove; (2) turn on the stove; (3) when the food is ready take it off; (4) finally, turn the stove off.

These are very simple steps that you can think up immediately, but the second step reminds you to think about each part. Don't just habitually do them without giving any thought to what you are doing.

You must now be sure that you will turn the stove off in the proper order called for here. This is where the third principle comes in. Make an extra step in this task that must be performed to remind you of the final step of turning off the stove. For this extra step let us say that we must place the food on the counter after removing it from the stove. Each time you place the food on the counter you should think of turning the stove off. Once you place the food down, immediately turn off the stove, don't do anything else first. This will solve the problem of forgetting to turn it off, but will you remember that you did later? To resolve this problem, you must perform the fourth principle.

The fourth principle requires that you pause after turning off the stove and picture the dials in their off position. Go ahead and check all of them and then picture all of them off. If later the thought should come to mind that you may not have turned the stove off or that some other dial might be still on, you will immediately recall to mind this picture of all of the dials actually being off.

Think how this can help you in your job and other areas of your life. Start practicing these principles and you can forget about absentmindedness!

# 6.

# MEDITATION – THE ART OF THINKING

In the last chapter we saw that many people consider absentmind-edness to be a problem with memory. In reality, though, the root of the problem is with the thinking process. I would now like to show you how to greatly improve your thinking ability through meditation. Just as many are mistaken about absentmindedness, so are many mistaken about what meditation is and how it can be employed properly to increase our mental capacity.

## MEDITATION — THE TRUE CONCEPT

Meditation is not having a blank mind. So many practice, or have heard of, transcendental meditation in which one more or less clears his mind of thoughts.

This is totally the wrong view of meditation. Webster's Dictionary says that to meditate is to think about, to contemplate; to reflect upon.

The correct view of meditation is the very opposite of having a blank mind. It means that we use our minds to think. We must fill our minds with thoughts. It is having active control over our minds and of what is being thought.

Meditation is thinking a subject through to a conclusion. It is working out solutions to problems. It is being able to collect your thoughts on a subject and prove a point. It is being creative, thinking about possible alternatives for resolving a problem or accomplishing a given task. True meditation is goal oriented and has a specific direction in mind.

## RAPID NOTES

When you think deeply about a subject, why waste your thoughts? A while later they are forgotten or are only vague at the most. Learn to take notes when you meditate on a subject. Since we think rapidly, we need a quick method for recording our thoughts and to be able to record them in an orderly form.

One such method for doing this is to use a circular outline technique. There are two ways to employ this outline technique depending on your purpose. If your purpose is to brainstorm a subject, or be creative, then you must use the *creative circular outline* form. If you want to develop a story flow, or think through a subject in a logical fashion, then you must use the *local circular outline* form.

## CREATIVE CIRCULAR OUTLINE

Let us first describe the creative circular outline approach. It may help to refer to the diagram of a creative outline in exhibit #11 as you read this explanation. With this technique you would begin with a subject or theme in mind. Write out a subject in a word or short phrase in the middle of your paper and circle it. In this example I am working with the subject of meditation. Now allow ideas to come into your mind that relate in some way to this subject word or phrase. As they come to mind quickly jot them down in a word or phrase around this large circle. Draw a short line out to this new word or phrase from this circle. Continue to jot down the thoughts that come to mind around this large center circle. Always connect each thought to the large circle. It is important to remember not to reject any thoughts that come to mind. You are trying to be creative so write down any related thought that comes to mind.

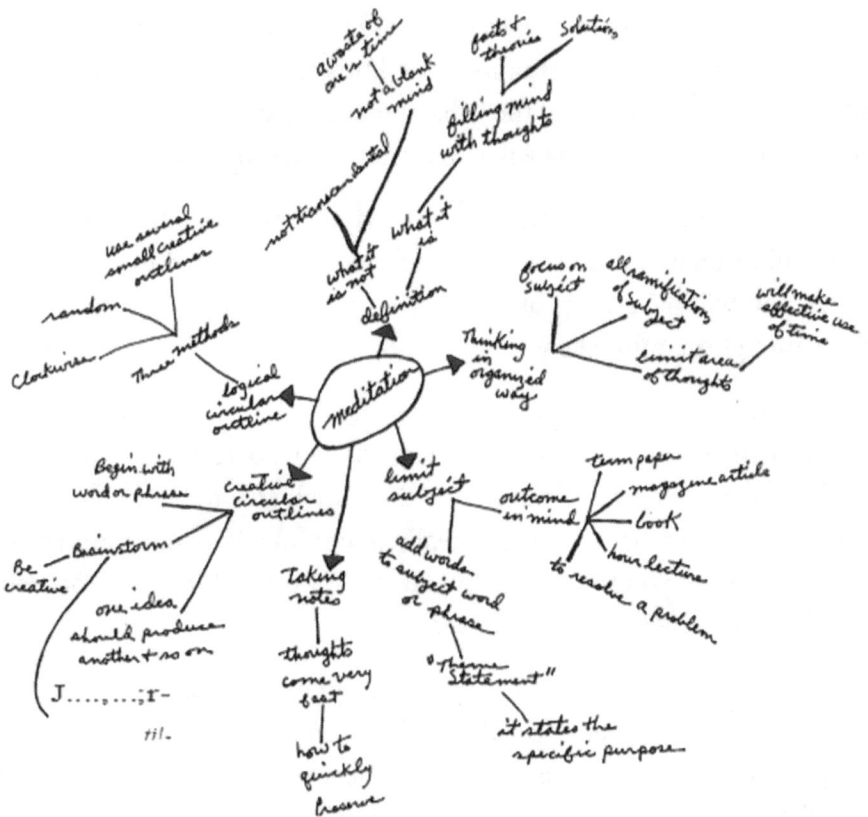

Exhibit #11

When these ideas are exhausted begin allowing ideas to come into mind about these offshoot thoughts. When a thought about one of these ideas come to mind, a short line out from the idea that prompted this thought. If your new thought triggers another one, just draw a short line out from it and write in the new thought. Continue with this process wherever a new thought arises. You will automatically see relationships. Several lines can imminate from each written thought or idea, and the lines do not have to be straight. Draw them any way that is convenient for getting the thoughts and relationships down on paper. An offshoot thought may trigger several separate ideas. Continue until all new ideas are exhausted. You will have developed all kinds of relationships of ideas pertaining to your subject word or phrase that was placed in the center of the page. You have now brainstormed this subject and have recorded all possible ramifications of the subject matter that you were aware of in your mind. You now know what you know about this subject.

By the time that you have exhausted all new thoughts about the ideas subordinate to the main ideas which are connected to the center circle, you will have probably developed a sense of direction in which these thoughts could take you.

You will automatically see a theme on which to think more deeply and in an organized manner. In other words, you now have eliminated in your mind many of the offshoot thoughts which are on this paper as not being related to what you would really like to meditate on thoroughly. This will enable you to boil down your topic. You will then be focused on what is pertinent to your subject.

At this time, you should write out a statement that will limit the subject to a manageable portion. This statement gives the specific purpose for the meditation or speech or lecture, or article or whatever it is that you will develop. It tells exactly what you will think or write about and no more. We will be referring to this statement of the specific purpose as the Theme Statement or TS. You will have now limited the subject, which was very general and large in scope, to a theme that is specific and is much smaller in scope. The scope of the theme will depend on what you will do with the information derived from this exercise of meditation. Are you going to prepare an hour lecture or speech; will you write out a short article or term paper on this subject matter; or are you just interested in resolving a problem?

## LOGICAL CIRCLE OUTLINE

You are now ready to begin developing logical thoughts about your Theme Statement. To do this you will use the logical circle outline form. There are three ways to develop a circular logical outline once you have decided on a Theme Statement. There is the clockwise method, the random method, and the method of using several small creative circular outlines. I will discuss the clockwise method first. (See Exhibit #12)

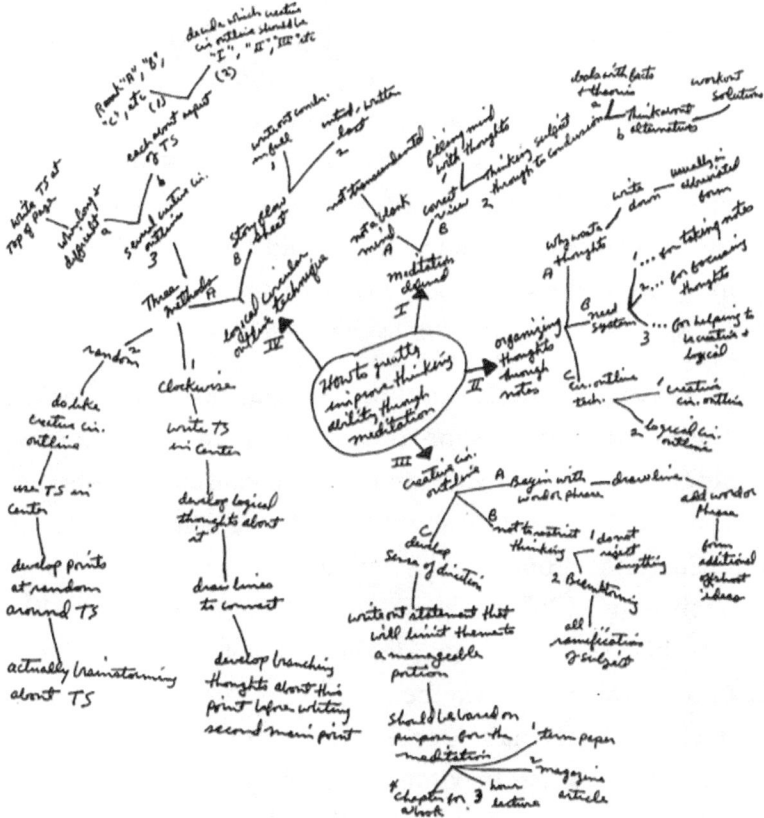

Exhibit #12

Start a new page, write out your Theme Statement or a short form of it in the center of the page and circle it with a large circle. You should write out the TS in full on a separate sheet of paper. This will be only the first of several ideas that must be written on this paper. We will refer to it as the Story Flow Sheet from now on. Do this for all of these methods described here. Now you will direct your thoughts to this limited theme of the subject with which you began earlier.

Allow thoughts on this Theme Statement to come to mind. With this circular outline form, you will begin at one location of the circle and continue around clockwise with main points about the Theme Statement. However, you will develop the branches off of this first main point before writing the second main point off from the large circle. Write these subpoints of the first main point completely first. Be sure to draw a short line from the main point to these newly added ideas. As before you may have several offshoots from this first main point. Just continue to branch thoughts and connect them with short lines until you know what the next main point should be. Remember, you may use as many short lines from any idea that you need. When no more thoughts come to mind, move on to the next.

With this logical circular outline, you will think each main point through in all of its details before proceeding on to the next main point concerning the TS. When you complete this outline, you should have a natural story flow of ideas about this Theme Statement. When you finish the first main point, label it with a Roman numeral "I" and label each branch with "A", "B", "C", etc. See how it is done in exhibit #12. After you finish with the second main idea and all of it branches, label it with a Roman numeral "II" and do the same as above with the subpoints as they branch off of this main idea. Do this for every main point and all subordinate points when they branch. If you have several subordinate points that simply follow one behind the other without branching, do not bother to label with letters and numerals. Only label where branches occur because later when you want to go over these ideas in your mind or you want to put these ideas down on paper you will want to know the story flow of what point comes next. This labeling method will do this automatically for you.

The random method should be used when you have developed the Theme Statement, but you are not sure about what you will say. You will need to brainstorm the Theme Statement.

The creative circular outline form is the technique I have shown you for brainstorming so that is how you should begin. The difference here is that you will begin with the Theme Statement in the center of the page with a circle around it instead of just a subject word or phrase of two or three words.

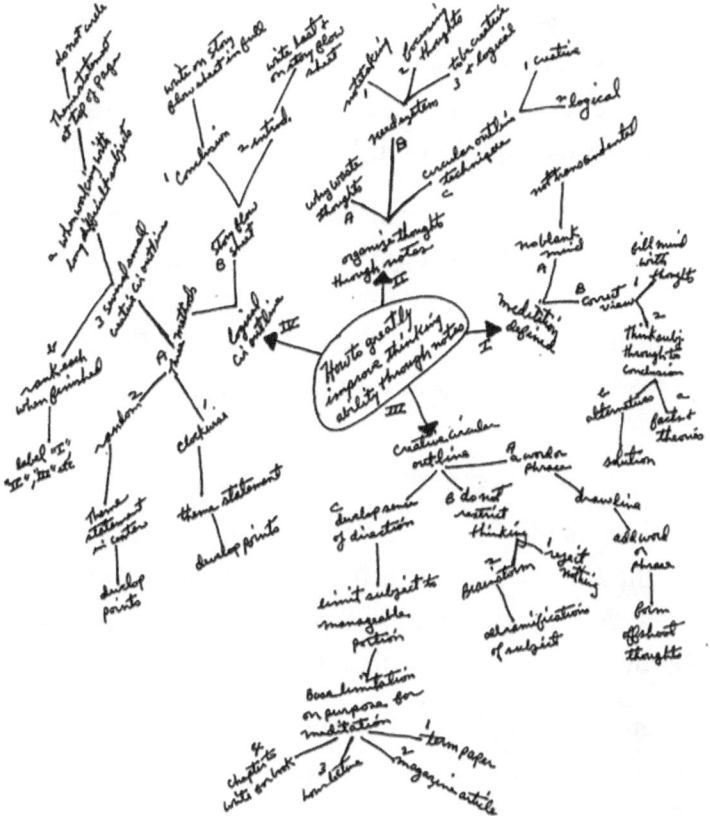

Exhibit #13

It works the same way though from this point on. Just jot down any words and phrases that come to mind about this TS. Write them at any position around the center circle. You are simply allowing the ideas about the TS to flow. Once you feel that you have all of those ideas written down around this center circle, you may begin developing offshoot ideas subordinate to them.

Once all of the offshoot ideas cease coming to mind, you must begin thinking about how to organize these points. The details are now present for each of the main points located closest to the center circle. Since everything is present that you would need for developing a logical circular outline, why waste your time redoing it? Why not just order these main points with Roman numerals to indicate which will come first, which would come second etc.? Once you do this you will in effect have a logical circular outline. See exhibit #13. This was the second method. Now let me explain a third method.

In the third method we can use several small creative circular outlines. We will need to use this when we are dealing with a very long or difficult subject. As in the other two methods just explained, you will have already developed your Theme Statement. This time, however, write it at the top of this page and do not circle it.

Each small creative outline will be about some facet or aspect of the Theme Statement. Therefore, it is a facet or aspect of the Theme Statement that should be circled in the center of each small creative circular outline. Since there will be several facets or aspects to your Theme Statement, there will be several creative circular outlines. Develop each individual outline first.

Once you have completed the brainstorming of each of these facets or aspects you will need to convert each outline to a logical circular outline form. Place a capital letter by the main ideas of each small creative circular outline so that it will be transformed into a logical circular outline.

Finally, decide which small logical circular outline should come first, which should come second etc. Place a Roman numeral "I" in the center circle of the circular outline that you feel should be first. Continue numbering until all of the circular outlines have Roman numerals indicating their desired order. This order should work well with the Theme Statement that you have written out at the top of the page. See exhibits 14a, 14b, and 14c for a clearer understanding of this method.

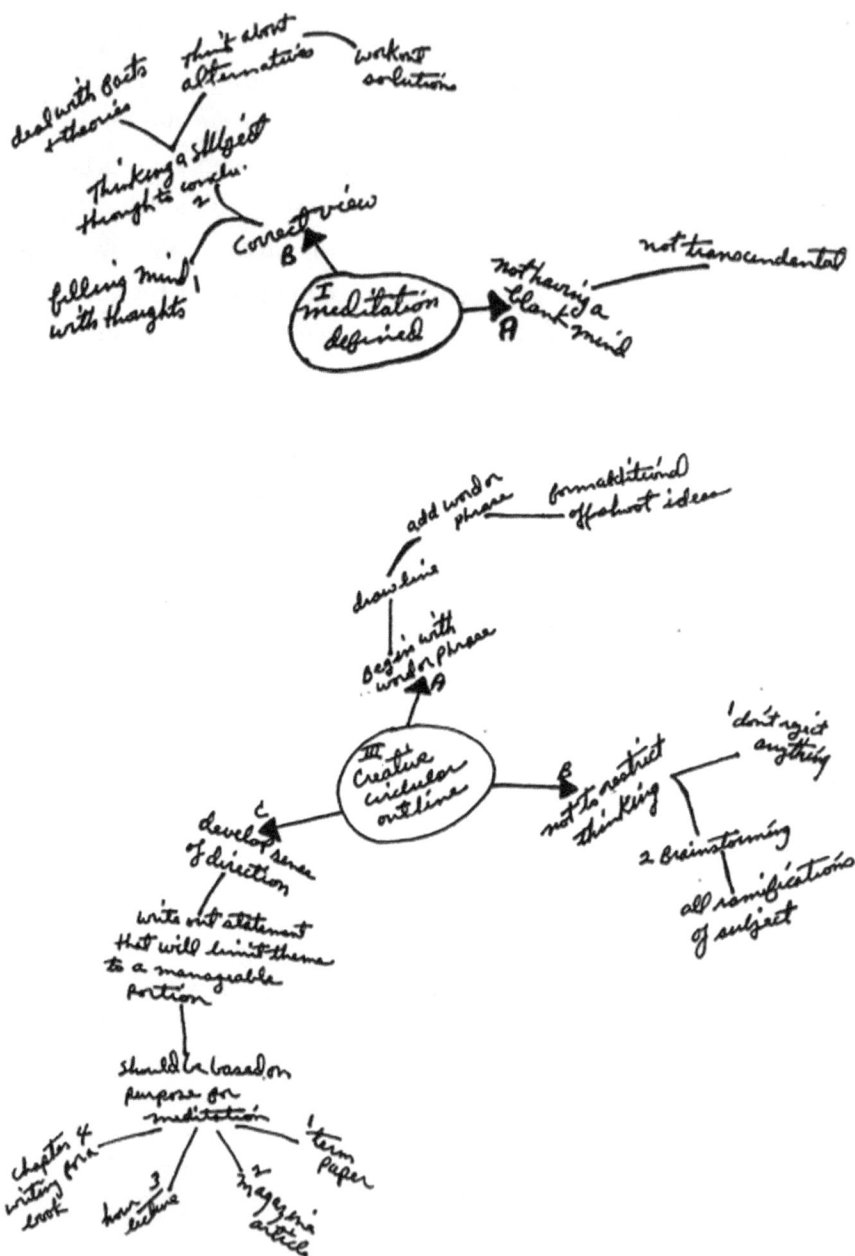

Exhibit 14a

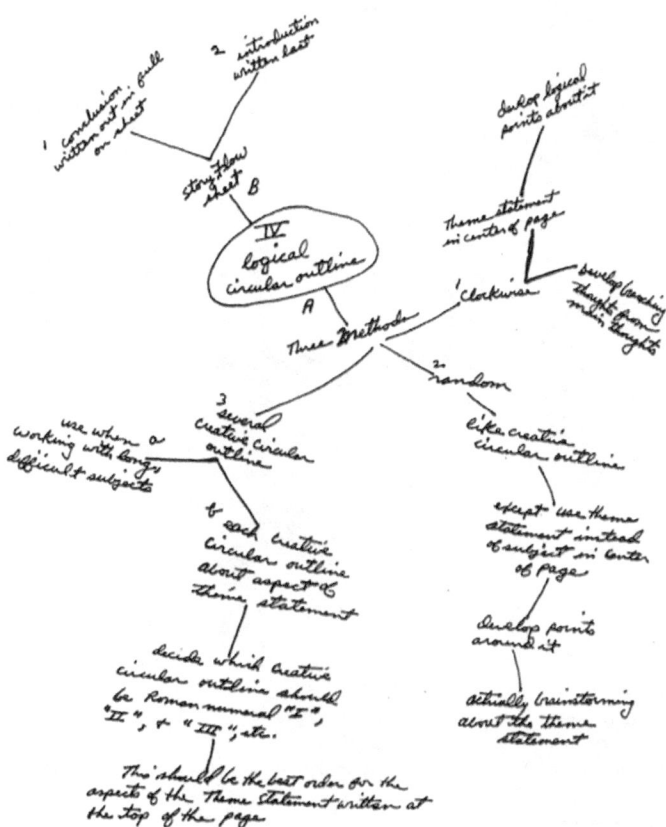

Exhibit #14b

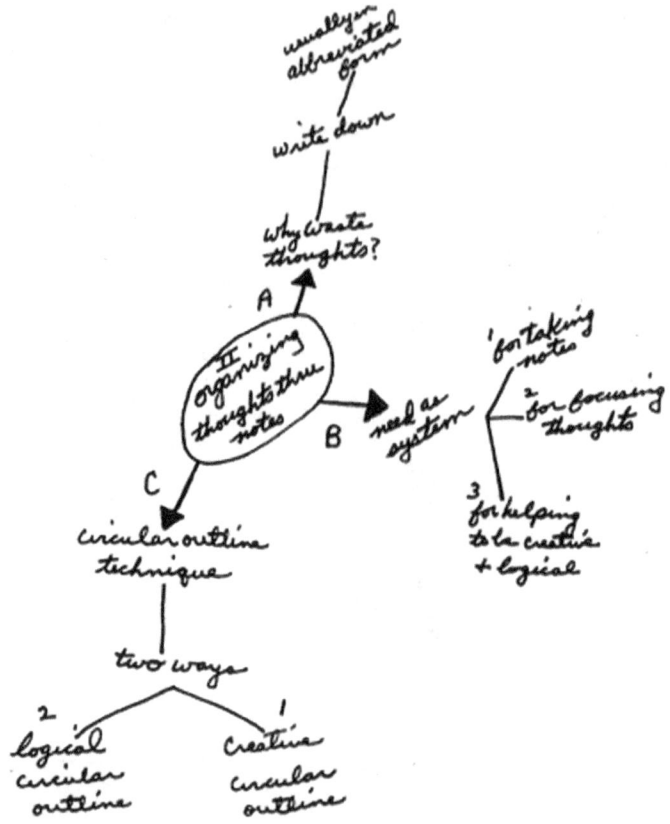

Exhibit #14c

I have explained these different methods so that you will be able to be flexible. Different situations will call for different approaches. Do what is comfortable for you. The conclusion reached after thinking a subject through should be written afterwards on another sheet of paper that we referred to earlier as the Story Flow Sheet and not on the logical circular outline. Also, this conclusion should include a sentence that is a restatement of the Theme Statement in some form. It should not be word for word but at least a reference to it.

The introduction should be written last after you know what you have discussed. I will explain more about the introduction in chapter VII.

# 7.

# PREPARING A SPEECH

Meditation, as discussed in chapter VI, is the basis for preparing a good speech. In this chapter we will see how to convert the notes from your meditation into a speech in its final form for delivery.

Before converting it into a speech, however, we need to know what the main parts of a speech are and their distinct purposes. A speech is basically divided into three main parts or sections: an introduction, a body, and a conclusion.

## PARTS OF A SPEECH

The purpose of the introduction is to grab the attention of the audience. It must be interesting. It can be made interesting and exciting by relating a humorous incident in connection with the theme of the speech. The speaker could also ask a challenging question or even a series of attention-getting questions that he will be answering in his speech.

Most importantly though an introduction should tell the audience the purpose for this speech. It should tell them what the speech will be about. This will enable the audience to follow the main points of the speech more easily. The specific purpose of the speech should be stated in one sentence that we call the Theme Statement. This sentence should come at the end of the introduction just before beginning the body.

Sometimes this Theme Statement is held until the conclusion. In this case, all of the main points must lead up to this conclusion. This should be rarely used and then only by experienced speakers.

After the introduction of a speech comes the body. The body gives the main points which are developed by many subpoints and their details. These main points are the original branches on your logical circular outline developed while meditating. The subpoints and their details are the other branches and offshoots from these first branches.

There should be transitional sentences in the body of a speech to give continuity. They should be located at the beginning or end of each main point to carry the listener from one main point to the next smoothly. They help keep the idea of organization in the listeners' minds. They help avoid confusion of points.

There should be one after the introduction to begin the body and the first main point. Another should be between the first main point and the second. This transitional sentence could be the last sentence of the first main point or the first sentence of the second main point.

If the transitional sentence is the last sentence of the first main point, you will be saying in essence that I have finished the first point and we are going to the next one. If it is the first sentence of the second main point, you will in essence be saying that you have finished the first main point and we are beginning the second. It is simply a matter of viewpoint according to the speaker. Continue doing this until you come to the conclusion. Here your transitional sentence will have reference in some way to the Theme Statement at the end of the introduction.

All of these transitional sentences plus the Theme Statement should be on your *Story Flow Sheet* before you begin writing the speech out.

The conclusion of the speech should be so well thought out that it should be obvious to your audience. By stating a conclusion sentence at the beginning of it that reflects on the Theme Statement, your audience will be advised that this is the conclusion of your speech. You should avoid saying such phrases as "in conclusion" to notify your audience that you have reached this point of the speech.

The conclusion of the speech should give the sense of a definite stopping point. It should fix the purpose or objective of the speech in the minds of the audience. If you called for any action to be taken in your speech then you should definitely take this time to stir them to that action.

## DEVELOPING SPEECH

Just knowing the parts of a speech and their purposes is not enough. We must learn to systematically put these parts together so that there is a natural story flow of ideas from the introduction to the conclusion. Remember in chapter VI we began our meditation with a creative circular outline.

With this technique we were able to investigate a subject. We received ideas in our minds at random as we concentrated on the subject. The term most often used for this is brainstorming.

After working with this creative circular outline, we focused in on a certain direction of thoughts that we had uncovered during this exercise. We then had to compose a Theme Statement and write it in brief phrases in the center of a blank sheet of paper. Also, we had to write the Theme Statement out in its fullest form on the Story Flow Sheet. This was the beginning of a logical circular outline. We then developed the main points of the body of the speech. We began branching from these main points to build subordinate points and related details.

After developing the main points, we could arrive at a conclusion. Now to state the conclusion you should start thinking of the Theme Statement and develop a sentence that draws a conclusion and at the same time relates back to the Theme Statement of the speech. It is a restatement of the Theme Statement. You may have to add some words to this sentence to make the transition from the body. This gives the speech a sense of completeness. You began with a specific purpose for giving your speech and ended with that specific purpose being fulfilled. This is what the conclusion should say. Be sure to write the full conclusion which should include this sentence on the Story Flow Sheet.

So far, we have the Theme Statement and the FULL conclusion written out on the Story Flow Sheet. This full conclusion includes a sentence that is a restatement of the Theme Statement that will be included in the full introduction when it will be written on the Story Flow Sheet. Now we must write transitional sentences for each main point on this *Story Flow Sheet* also.

To create these transitional sentences, you will need to look at your logical circular outline. From it you can see what the speech is about and the main points that will be brought out. You will need to make the first transitional sentence to start the body of the speech. Then you will make others to link the main points together into one perfect whole. Write these on your *Story Flow Sheet* after the conclusion (The conclusion on the *Story Flow Sheet* is written out in full.)

Sometimes you may feel that a long sentence is necessary to convey the idea of a particular transitional sentence. In this case you might consider breaking it up into two shorter ones. The two sentences together will convey the same meaning but will appear simpler.

At this point you will need to write the introduction on your Story Flow Sheet. It is only after you have completed your logical circular outline and have written your conclusion in full on the *Story Flow Sheet* along with the transitional sentences that you will be able to write an appropriate interest-getting introduction. You have to know what will be said in the speech before you can introduce it.

You should now be able to read over the *Story Flow Sheet* and see that your speech is one complete whole. There is a logical story flow from the beginning of the introduction unto the end of the conclusion.

The order that you will have the information listed on your *Story Flow Sheet* will be this: the Theme Statement, the full conclusion, the transitional sentences that will appear between the main points, and the full introduction. The order in which to read over the *Story Flow Sheet* to see that it truly does make a complete whole from the introduction to the conclusion is this: The introduction which will include the Theme Statement, the transitional sentences between the main points, and then the conclusion which will include the conclusion sentence that is a restatement of the Theme Statement in the introduction.

## FINAL FORM

The next task is to write the speech out in its final form for delivery. There are two basic ways to write out a speech. The speaker will either use an outline to speak from or a manuscript with the entire speech typed out word for word. If you plan to use an outline it is not necessary that you write the speech out word for word, but some speakers may wish to write it out word for word and then put it in outline form for delivery.

1. At this juncture I would like to briefly go over some very general principles for typing the speech up in manuscript form. Your introduction has been written on the *Story Flow Sheet* so merely copy it over on the paper on which you intend to write your rough draft. With the introduction typed on your rough draft, you may now proceed to the body of the speech.

Here you begin typing it up from the logical circular outline thought for thought. If additional thoughts come to mind, write them out on your rough draft too. Try to sound conversational in your writing. Also be sure to refer to the Story Flow Sheet to obtain your transitional sentences to be used when starting the body and in between main points.

When you have completed the body, you only need to copy the conclusion that you have previously written up on your Story Flow Sheet on to your rough draft and you have your speech.

Of course, you will have to review it for errors and for changes that you would like to make. This is just your rough draft, but basically this will be your speech.

2. If, on the other hand, speaking from a manuscript is not for you, I will discuss the steps for developing a vertical outline from which to speak. Since you have already written out your introduction, you merely outline it in phrases that will help you recall what needs to be said when delivering the speech. This is not a formal outline but a working outline. Freely write reminders that will help you remember your thoughts out to the side of phrases or place them in parentheses. When you finish outlining the introduction, proceed to outline the body in this same fashion.

The points to be outlined will come from the logical circular outline. Outline vertically thought for thought from the circular outline. Write them, of course, in the order in which you plan to say them. If additional thoughts come to mind and bare on the subject matter being discussed, go ahead and include them in your outline at the appropriate place. Remember to use phrases rather than sentences.

To aid in writing out a Vertical Outline you may want to number the order of points and subpoints on the logical circular outline.

Number the main points with Roman numerals. At the next fork or where several branches emanate from a circled main idea, you will be able to use capital letters. The next time use Arabic numerals. Finally, if needed, you can use small case letters too.

With this information and techniques, you will be able to convert your meditations into speeches and into their final form for delivery.

# 8.
# READING TECHNIQUES THAT MAKE A DIFFERENCE

You have now been shown how to improve your memory, your ability to think even how to write a speech, but I feel that there is still one more important technique that I should discuss — that is the reading technique. In this chapter I would like to explain a five-step method for handling reading assignments that will help you read faster and learn more quickly. I call it the SR3 S Method.

## SURVEY

The first step is to survey what you plan to read. This is just to get an overall view of the organization and an idea of what the theme will be. This will be handled a little differently each time depending on whether you will be reading a book, a chapter of a book, or an article in a magazine.

1.  If the reading material is a book, you should begin by looking over the table of contents. This will quickly give you an idea of what will be covered in the book in a general way by reading all of the chapter titles. It will also allow you to see the basic overall organization of the material to be read.

Secondly, you will need to take a look at the index. Just glance through it and notice the subjects to be covered by the book.

The next procedure to take before beginning to read a book is to look over charts and maps that catch your eye as you flip through the pages of the book. Be sure to read the captions. Sometimes valuable information is given there.

The last thing to do is to find the Theme Statement in the book.

Now if you were planning to only be reading a chapter in a text book at this time, how could you get a quick survey of it? First of all, read the chapter title. This will indicate what the theme of the chapter could be.

Be sure to look at chapter graphs and maps.

Next locate the TS in the introduction to the chapter.

Then, read all of the section headings if there are any, and continue by reading all of the bold print headings and subheadings. Go through the entire chapter in this way first. Don't read anything else at this time.

2.  Now go back to the beginning of the chapter and begin reading the first sentence of each paragraph. Read the details of each paragraph only if the sentence is about the theme of the chapter or about the bold print heading above the paragraph. This tells you that the details will be about these themes and not some irrelevant point or points. In this way you will be able to cut your way through a lot of reading material quickly and read only relevant information concerning the theme of the chapter which is what should be important to you. If this is just some personal reading, this may be all you need to do. You may find all that you would be interested in and not have to read the chapter word for word at all. Of course, if this is assigned reading for class you better go on and read it word for word.

Finally, before beginning the actual reading step, look in the back of the chapter and read over any questions there. Do not try to answer them. Just read them so you will know what the author expects you to find out through reading the chapter. You might like to jot down key words and phrases on a piece of paper to remind you what to be looking for as you read.

3. We would survey a magazine article differently than we would a book or a chapter of a book. First, look at all pictures and charts and read all captions. This will give you a taste of what to expect. Then locate the TS probably in the introduction.

Secondly, read all of the bold print headings. This will give you an idea of the organization of the article. You should be able to see the story flow of the article before you begin reading word for word.

## READ

The second letter of the acrostic is R3. This actually represents three "R's". The first "R" stands for "reading". Many people are interested in speed reading. Let me show you a quick, easy way to increase you reading speed dramatically. Simply hold your pen or pencil above the page as you move it from left to right quickly as if you were underscoring the line you are reading. You are not drawing a line on the paper, however. Your pen or pencil is not touching at all. Just keep it very close to touching as you guide it across the page.

What you are doing is using this as a pacer. Draw it back and forth across the page under what you are reading. Push for speed by making the pencil or pen travel faster than you can normally read. Set a goal for completing what you want to read. Count how many pages and figure up a time limit for what you have to do. Push yourself to reach your goal. Keep doing this and try to go faster each time you read until you reach a level with which you are satisfied. You can easily double you reading speed using this method.

What about important information that you find as you are reading? In order to keep up your speed you cannot stop to ponder points or to try to get a better understanding of some concept. This is not the proper time. So, what do you do? Mark the passage quickly with a vertical line in the margin next to the beginning and ending of the sentences, depending on whether the margin is on the left or right of the sentences. This is much quicker and neater than underlining sentences. Continue to read. Your goal is to get through the reading material that you have set as your goal. After your reading is complete, you should return to these marked passages and label them with a key word or phrase in the margin beside the vertical line.

Under this "R" standing for "reading", we have discussed speed reading and how to mark passages without hindering your speed. Now, I would like to discuss indexing. When you label a marked passage that you think may be important enough to want to find again later, you should index it. It is important that you do this at this time because you are most interested in what you are reading at the time you are reading it. Years later you may need this information but at that time you may not feel as interested. You will then be glad that you had already done some research work when you first read the book.

Here is how you index a book. List the subjects on the fly leaf of the book that would refer to passages that you have previously marked and labeled. Use only a key word or phrase to indicate the subject area. Out to the right jot down the page on which this marked passage is to be found. If you find more passages on that subject, just add their page numbers too separated by commas. Do not be concerned about order. Feel free to add any page number next. Make the system easy and practical for yourself. By indexing important subjects, you will be able to review the book quickly weeks, months, even years after having read it. If you are interested in obtaining some specific information and you know that it is contained in a book of yours that you have read and indexed, then you will be able to quickly look it up. This comes in handy when writing a research paper. You may save yourself many hours of work in a library making note cards. Each time you are able to use information indexed in a book you have in your own library, you have saved yourself the work of one or more note cards to be written in a library after taking time to find the material. It is even possible to write an entire research paper from your own books using the indexes that you have compiled in them as you read them originally.

## RECITE

The next step, or second "R", is to recite to yourself what you remember from the reading. After you have surveyed and read the material, find out what you remember about it and what you do not. To do this effectively you will need to use a creative circular outline.

Begin your creative circular outline by writing the Theme Statement or TS in the center of your paper and circle it. Proceed by jotting down outside around this center circle the key words and phrases that come to mind concerning what you read about this Theme or TS. Be sure to draw a line out from this center circle containing the Theme to the keywords or phrases that it brings to mind. Continue as long as this theme produces ideas for you. When your thoughts about this circled theme or TS cease coming to mind, start off-shoot thoughts. Be sure to draw a short line to these off-shoot thoughts and connect each off-shoot thought with a line to the previous thought that generated it.

Why do you need to do this? You need to because this will tell you what you remember and what you do not remember from your reading. Try to do this from memory at first. You may have to look back when you realize that some things are somewhat unclear or hazy in your mind at this point. Add to you outline whatever you feel is important.

This will give you a quick recitation of the material. From this you should be able to see where the difficult portions are. This then brings us to our next step that deals with understanding these more difficult portions.

## REVIEW

In this step you review over what you have read and what you have jotted down on your creative circular outline. Try to get an understanding about anything that seems puzzling at this time.

Reread portions slowly analyzing what you read. Look for principles. Ask yourself questions like, "what if this and that and the other were the case?" Study the material to see what the author is really saying and is trying to get across to you. Look up terms. Read related material in some other books or chapters of the book in which you are studying.

In addition to these suggestions try making smaller logical circular outlines concerning the difficult passages. Break the passages down. Think through what is stated here. Carry on a conversation with yourself about the main points and their details to get a fuller understanding of them.

Add any additional information that you find to your creative circular outline. Be sure to see how it relates so that you add it in the appropriate place.

## SYNTHESIZE

The last step is called synthesizing. This is the organizing step. Take a look at your creative circular outline. Look it over well and try to see a logical story flow with the ideas presented there. Once you see it, develop a logical circular outline. Refer back to chapter VI if you cannot recall how to develop the logical circular outline. As you continue developing this outline, refer to the reading material when necessary to obtain needed information. Try, as much as possible, to develop it just from the creative circular outline. You should have practically all of the information that you deemed important on the creative circular outline by now. Your logical circular outline after it is fully developed will bring everything together into a logical story flow. This will aid you in remembering the material. Remember that organization is a key to be able to remember a large amount of information. You may need to quickly convert this outline into a vertical outline for whatever purpose you may have. This is easily accomplished from this logical circular outline.

Now is the time to apply the memory techniques that I discussed in earlier chapters. Your natural memory has by now picked up a lot of details already just by virtue of having worked your way through this material in this systematic manner. Now all that you need to do is to organize these points and details to help you remember them. The memory techniques discussed in the earlier chapters will do just that for you.